The FIVE Fs *of* LIFE

TUAN TA

CONTENTS

I'd like to acknowledge the following people:

DARIUS KING
who taught me to question myself and show the facts

CUONG LIU
who showed me that not all Asians are physically weak

STAN CHIANG
who represents deep conviction with challenges

KRISTIN MASTERS *and* JENNIFER MCNEIL
who helped edit my first book

JULIE FAIRES
who designed the cover and layout

DAVID BULLOCK
who told me to just get it done

MY FAMILY
who is always with me even though I have doubts

INTRODUCTION

"Life is an opportunity; benefit from it.
Life is beauty; admire it.
Life is a dream; realize it.
Life is a challenge; meet it.
Life is a duty; complete it.
Life is a game; play it.
Life is a promise; fulfill it.
Life is sorrow; overcome it.
Life is a song; sing it.
Life is a struggle; accept it.
Life is a tragedy; confront it.
Life is an adventure; dare it.
Life is luck; make it.
Life is too precious; do not destroy it.
Life is life; fight for it. "

–MOTHER THERESA

If you are reading this now, you must be curious about the book, someone passed it on to you, or you want to learn how to balance your life. I have designed this book to be read in about 30 minutes and to be passed along to others who need it. Because we are so busy with everyday tasks, we tend to forget about the important things in life. Ever want to learn how to juggle multiple things, manage contradicting priorities, or simply get more time back? The book you have in your hands will change your life if you simply take action and keep learning.

Now I want you to imagine your life with all of your challenges. I bet it's filled with challenges. Well, my whole life has been a series of challenges as well. But in each challenge lies opportunity. Mother Theresa often reminded her brethren that nothing ever happens how we expect it to happen; and often we find opportunity, revelation, and promise where we expected to find only hardship, emptiness, and dead ends. She says it best when we are talking about the game of life and faith.

Consequently, my faith has enabled me to see that one cannot predict or control one's life. But my experiences have given me insight into what is truly important. While living in Nashville, Tennessee, I experienced a transformation–unexpected, as such experiences usually are. I never thought I would come to discover such deep faith in this place.

As my faith in God has grown, so has my personal philosophy. Through this short book, I hope to share the lessons I have learned through my walk with God. Just like everyone, I have reached crossroads in my life; indeed, every day presents us with new choices and decisions to make. I hope this philosophy will provide solace and guidance to others who seek to improve their faith and their lives. My earnest wish is to help everyone to find success and happiness.

The key to that success is a simple principle called the Five Fs: Faith, Fitness, Family, Friends, and Finances. These five topics are easy to remember, yet each one plays a critical role in one's success. Achieving balance in these five areas means achieving balance in one's priorities, which is central to a successful, happy life.

The sequence of the Five Fs is important. When I originally conceived the Five Fs, the order was different: Faith, Family, Friends, Fitness, and Finances. Then I visited the doctor and received shocking news. As I heard the results of my physical, realization struck: if I cannot take care of myself, how can I expect to care for my family? After that doctor's visit, I placed Fitness before Family, to reflect the importance of self-care and health. Please do not take this priority to a point where you are neglecting your family. Remember you need to balance the Five Fs, but whatever you focus on you will improve the quickest.

My goal is to present the Five F's simply and briefly, so that anyone can understand and put them into practice for a life that is worth living. There is no point in having all the money in the world if you can't spend it, or a family to love and never receive love back. I hope that you will bring the Five Fs into your life, because life is too short to waste God's wonderful gifts to the world. I want to challenge you to ask questions and not just accept the knowledge from this book because you will not appreciate it enough to see the value.

FAITH

MAIN POINTS
- What? Faith is firm belief in something for which there is no proof by definition.
- Why? Without Faith, there lies ambiguity with life.
- When? Have faith all the time, not only when you need it.
- Where? Everywhere
- How? Pray, mediate, contemplate, surround yourself with the right people

"Faith is believing in things when common sense tells you not to."
—GEORGE SEATON

Before we begin, I want you to think of a positive moment in your life when you were the most happy or excited. For me, it was a day during the summer of 2003 when I was sitting on the beach. At that moment, I was happy because I knew I had reached one of my goals in life. Whatever that moment is for you, keep that thought in your mind first. What I am doing is preparing your mind to receive the knowledge it took me many years of reading and living to understand.

11

The cornerstone of the Five F's is Faith. What is faith? It is the enduring belief that a higher being exists, who is with us in times of joy, sorrow, and everything in between. Without faith in God first, faith in ourselves is not enough.

What if you don't have faith? In that case, is there a point to read on if you do not know what you final destination is? I believe faith also encompasses believing that you have a purpose in your life besides merely living. I stopped believing in coincidence because I have faith that things happen for a reason. For example, the fact that you are reading my book shows that many circumstances had to happen for you to read it. You could have received the book, bought it, found it or obtainied it by whatever means. But on my side there are a lot of circumstances that led me to write the book. I am sure if we asked a mathematician he or she would say the odds of this book being written and distributed would be highly unlikely. But yet we are here together.

Let's take a walk through history. There were many people who died throughout history for their faith. Why was it so important? Simply, they could not live a lie to themselves. Think about Joan of Arc, Martin Luther King, Jr., or Gandhi. Each one went on to live with faith that they were doing right actions. As a result, they were convicted to their faith regardless of the consequences even death.

It was faith that brought Mother Teresa to India to help impoverished people. It was by faith that the Pilgrims decided to take a risky voyage to America, knowing that they could all perish. Every day, we have the faith that the sun will rise and fall within a 24-hour period. We believe the world will not end even with current economic troubles. Consequently, as I look back through history, I see many other moments where faith played a role in shaping the destiny of our civilization, e.g. putting a man on the moon.

Do you want to know what is the scariest part of faith? Failing to act on it. I used to think that missed opportunities were the scariest part of faith, but it simply is not the case. If you work hard at it, there are simply more opportunities. You just have to start somewhere. The real challenge for me is overcoming how, every day, we can live with ourselves without taking action (no matter how little).

Remember, we know how to lose weight or stop smoking, but we lack the faith that we can do it. We are willing to accept short-term pleasures in exchange for long-term loss. I wish I could inject faith into all of us (even myself at times), but it doesn't come from a magic pill. It comes from within you to simply believe.

If only there were a way to do this! I myself have lacked faith in the past. Of course, I still have my challenging moments like everybody else in the world. I did not accept this idea simply because someone told me. I went out and searched for the truth. The first thing I told myself was that I can't be the only one feeling this way. As a result, I have studied self-help books and successful people. What made the books so interesting? What made these people so great? What I have concluded is that they simply had faith they could do something while others lacked in that faith. You would typically hear from athletes, for example, that they simply close their eyes, and they can see themselves doing whatever they have to do. Is this true? It is true to a certain point. We are limited with our abilities. Please don't see yourself flying and jump out of the window! But we go through this process every day without too much thought. Do we hesitate seeing ourselves from getting to and from work? I think not.

The question for me is how this can be achieved. I surround myself with people and fill my brain with positive thoughts. I read biographies of great people. I imagine what they would do in my situations. I simply have the faith that the people who came before me had the same challenges in their lives and that they still figured out a way to do this.

By following and testing out this new-found faith, I grew stronger and stronger. As I grew stronger and stronger, I had to raise the bar of my faith because I had to let go of more things and trust that all things will happen for a reason. All I had to do was my part, believing and executing.

Everyone reaches a point where it's impossible to avoid making a tough choice. That's why it is important to continue to build your faith and never stop. When faced with a difficult situation, I was incredibly blessed, because it was in that moment that I knew my faith was being tested. I had to just give into the faith as so many books and people have said. Funny how when you stop trying so hard, things start to make sense. A clear, practical example would be getting a job.

What if you got your dream job, but you had to give up something? What if that something was your son's football game or daughter's dance recital? A lot of people would say, "Sure. Why not? By having a better job, I will be able to provide more for them." But the truth is that no matter how much money you have, you simply can't buy back that time. There lie the tough moments; you can't buy time. You can buy things. You can try to become creative, but in the end you will have to make some sort of decision. Having faith that things will work out is great. But we must act on our faith no matter how little.

Now I see that all my experiences were part of God's plan. I used to wonder why I was so different from my parents, especially when my behavior embarrassed them, or vice versa. But those experiences made me who I am today. For example, as a child I use to translate for my parents from Vietnamese to English for medical, legal, and other situations. I wondered why I had to endure this torture. The worst moment was when I was nine at the local hospital. They thought my mother had passed away and asked me to translate to my father what had happen. Fortunately, she did not pass away. It gave me a different perspective growing up. I said to myself as I got older that no nine-year-old should endure that situation. Years later, I volunteer at a clinic on a regular basis. Now I get a truly blessed opportunity to help families that in the same situation.

Is this some coincidence? Of course, you could argue I was simply in the right place at the right time with the right abilities. Again, I think there was a particular reason I had to experience what I did as a child. The result of that experience resulted in the ability to affect many families now. Think back to your own life for a moment. There must have been those moments when you realized you were able to help someone because of another experience you had in the past. Without that experience you could not have acted. Can you keep ignoring each experience as a coincidence? I think not, because there are too many. I think it's funny that for all of our ability to rationalized things, we ignore some of the most evident things in life just because we don't understand them.

For some reason in my life, the number 5 has appeared over and over again and I did not understand why. After trying to ignore the number's appearance on many occasions, I started to question why it showed up. At first, I thought about it. Maybe it's because we have five fingers or maybe it's because we can usually have no more than three to five points we can remember at one time. Eventually, I said to myself we have five fingers for a reason. Otherwise, we would have seven fingers on our hands! Even though I cannot explain the reason, I am able to have the faith enough to trust apply the concept. As a result, this book contains Five Fs because I simply applied what I found in life.

By now, I hope you have enough faith in God's divine plan for you. He is your greatest protector. He guides your actions and choices, to help you become who you are today and what you will be in the future.

Once you commit to trusting God's plan, it is easy to keep happy, positive thoughts. But really believing is the hard part. It's not like doing 50 pushups, or driving blind.

Don't know when God's plan is going to start? Well, it starts as soon as you make the decision for it to start.

FITNESS

- What? Making sure your body is working at peak performance
- Why? If you cannot take care of yourself, how can you take care of others?
- When? Start today and make it part of your life every day
- Where? At work, around your neighborhood, at a gym
- How? Look at a diet and exercise program, start walking 30 minutes a day

Flying home to Nashville from Philadelphia, I fell into conversation with a fellow traveler. A woman in her fifties, she spoke with wisdom and assurance during our chat. Finally I asked her, "What advice would you give your younger self, knowing what you know now?" Her answer deeply surprised me: the woman wished she had taken better care of her health. Although she obviously made enough money to afford the best medical care available, she still wished she had had a deeper respect for her body because no matter how much money you have later, you cannot buy back lost time.

The real wake-up call for me was when I got my physical report back when I was 26. Imagine getting a report back saying you were overweight, pre-diabetic, and pre-whatever else. It didn't really hit me until I saw it in writing; that made me think, I am really not taking care of myself. What happened? A few years ago, I was wearing a size 31 and now I am a size 36. You might know what I am talking about. I was determined to get my health under control.

Want to know the secret to losing weight? Diet and exercise. There is no magic pill or wonder drug. Let's face some facts first. About 64% of adults in the United States of America are overweight or obese. That is crazy considering there are people dying of hunger. Think about it! The real problem in the U.S. is that we have easy access to food and we simply do not exercise enough. We want fast food and cheap food because it is easier than alternative of making a good meal. People are busy working and are tired at the end of the day.

While living in France, I was able to lose weight because I had smaller portions and walked more. In the U.S., if you have a typical cube job, you would barely walk from meeting to meeting and then eat at your office. No matter how much you want to change, the environment is not allowing you to change. Consider also that our food in the U.S. has tons of sugar! As you can tell, the situation does not look good for the average American.

So what can I do? You can start small by simply walking and cutting back meal portions. The trick is to commit yourself to doing something rather than nothing. If you are like me, there are many times when I fail to kept my commitment because it's easy to not keep it. In order to be successful, I want you to make a plan.

If you are completely out of shape right now, I want you to stop whatever you are doing and make an action plan to change. Do not move on to the next part of the book until you have a plan. Please include your family and friends when you create the plan. I found that I can do this easier when I am doing it for other people. Therefore, put them at the top of list, or use whatever else is most important for you to motivate you to do this.

On another note, the best course of action is to prevent things from going bad. I want you to take out a calendar right now and mark off the dates to get physical, vision, and dental check ups. Also, have you considered taking advantage of your medical insurance programs? There are some programs that you can participate in that could lower your taxable income. One of these programs is called health savings account. It allows you to put money away for health spending.

If none of these has motivated you yet, I will speak in terms of monetary impact. The projected cost of health care is expected to grow four times over a typical lifetime in the U.S. I know what you must be thinking right now: what about the universal health care that is being enacted now? Again, remember the story of the woman on the plane: you cannot buy your health back. Please do not wait until the situation gets worse. It would be a shame for anyone to die because of things we can prevent. There are so many other things in the world to sacrifice for. But not taking care of yourself is not one of those things.

Our health has a huge impact on what we are able to accomplish and how well we can enjoy life. Preserving our health enables us to make the most of life. Furthermore, taking care of our bodies is a way of honoring God for the gifts and abilities He has given us. No one else can take care of your body except for you! Do not make excuses. Consider the short- and long-term effects of not eating right and exercising. Think about how those effects could get in the way of your dreams. Encourage yourself when you want to eat that extra dessert or make a trip to Starbucks.

FAMILY

MAIN POINTS

- What? Be an active member of your family
- Why? You only have one family
- When? Whenever you don't think there will be a second chance—always
- Where? In your heart and mind
- How? Be the best you can be when you are with them and from afar.

Family is foundational to a happy life because our family is there to share in our successes and support us in our trials. It is true that we cannot choose our family, but believe you were brought into that family for a particular reason. It's easy to say, "If only I was born in the other family, my life would be better." The truth is you do not know if life would be better or not. Everyone's family has problems whether they are small or big. What's important is that you have a family. If do not have a family, you are not alone either. Go find or make that family. You need not be alone in the world.

I had never realized how important family was until I visited

Vietnam when I was 25. My parents and I had left Vietnam when I was a baby, and I had never met my extended family. Let's think about this: my parents had to leave their families to find a better life not knowing if that was even possible. But yet after all these years, they went back. Why? There must be more to life than just our jobs and hobbies.

It was truly humbling to meet them for the first time. There in Vietnam, I realized what I had missed; I could never make up that time, or enjoy those long-lasting relationships. I made the most of that time in Vietnam and took the lesson back to the States with me. It was easy to see that my time there was limited, but I realized that our time with all our families is limited. Making the most of that time is critical.

Let's think about what keeps us away from our families for a moment. I am sure you will say that your job or business does that. "I would not be a good father or mother if I did not provide my family." It is true that we need to provide for our families, but our families cannot be placed on pause. But is your job and business so important that you'd neglect your family? I would ask myself to find a better way to earn a living. Don't end up a job that just pays the bills. Paying the bills will keep you away from your family. You deserved better because we have the opportunity in the U.S. to make a difference with our lives.

Make a decision today to put your family before a job or business. Otherwise, the book would have been the Four Fs + a J for job. It doesn't make sense to give up your family unless your family does not mean anything for you. The real trick is to make sure your family KNOWS you care about them by being there at the right moments in time. You will know the right moments in time. If you don't, here are some basic situations.

If you have children, take them to sports events, cultural events, and family picnics. Basically, give them the opportunity to learn and grow. My parents did not have a huge budget, but I learned from reading books. Books are free in a public library. For your significant other, take them out as if for the first time. Do things that will encourage your love for one another because in the end of our lives, we really only have our reputations, our faith and family to support us.

One thing that helps me the most is to try to picture a perfect family for me. The trick is not to stress when things don't happen exactly as planned. But the important thing is to learn from those situations in order to grow and to become better. Don't give up on your family either. For them to be there for you, you need to be there for them. As a matter of fact, when I feel down I think of my family because of the opportunity they have given me. Without them, I could not be pushing.

Our families play such an important role in our growth and development. It is families—in all shapes and sizes—that form the building blocks of society. Keeping your family life in order helps keep the rest of your life in order—at work, with friends, in the community. You MUST believe in the integrity and importance of your family.

FRIENDS

MAIN POINTS

- What? Having friends
- Why? Having someone to listen to you when they are not your family, but almost are
- When? For moments of joy and moments of sorrow
- Where? In parks, parties, beach
- How? In everything you do

Without Friends, how can we create moments in our lives that we won't forget? Friends are critical to the formula because they can give us a different perspective from our family, and especially from ourselves. Friends balance our perceptions, share interests, and bring humor to our lives.

I can say I have many friends in my life, but it is all relative. Some people require more friends than others, while others just need a few very good ones. I have found that friends are everywhere, though. I believe people are good in nature even though we see horrible things in the world constantly. I had asked one of my co-workers before he retired what amazed him about people. He said the greatest thing—and the worst-- he witnessed was the human heart. I thought about it; even though I had friends who created conflict with me for whatever reason, it was part of being human. We make mistakes. We all feel guilty, ashamed, proud, happy, sad, etc. We need to remember that the true part of being a friend is learning to forgive one another for past transgressions. Otherwise, we never really let go of our anger towards them.

Everyone says friends will support you no matter what the situation. But I've found the best friends are the ones who will disagree with you. It would be worse that a friend merely agrees with you simply to agree. Friends will tell you the truth regardless, but you need to take into consideration they can be wrong too. Remember to understand the situation first. Look for the friend who has always been honest with you, not the one who just agrees with you. When things really count, call on the friend who will tell the truth even if it might hurt. That's the only way I have found I can resolve anything. As a matter of fact, I have developed something called the "Sacred Five": the five people whom you could call no matter what happens. For example, if you were stuck in a third-world country and needed to get out or if you are falsely accused, whom would you call to help bail you out? Even with a large list of friends you would probably only contact five people because those five are the ones who can help you.

How can you tell a good friend from a bad friend? The answer is it that takes time to test your friends. Want a quick test? Check out your friend's MySpace, Facebook page, etc... The page will tell you a little about them. It will tell you if they have a lot of "friends" or a few "friends." There is no formal process, but there is a method. And hope is not a method to test your friends. The test is different from friend to friend, and so is what you would like test among your friends. For me, integrity is the biggest test. Integrity is doing the right things when no one is looking. It is not easy for an individual to achieve, but I believe the pursuit of it is still essential. You must consider the spirit of your friend's intentions. You will know what to do depending on the need. If not, ask a friend to help you! But the focus should be constant evaluation throughout time. Situations don't make good or bad friends, they show good or bad friends.

In today's era, it is so easy to make a friend. Due to websites like Facebook, MySpace, Meetups etc., we can be connected socially even without being physically there. It does bring a new paradigm shift. Have you noticed how different people communicate in different manners? For example, people sometimes communicate by e-mail, text message, or by phone ONLY. How strange is it that although people have access to all these technologies, they choose to use only certain ones? I believe this trait derives from personality and culture. From my personal experience, I test friends out what method is the best way for each of them. Try every one until one seems to work better than another. Don't think about the golden rule, because you need to treat your friends the way they want to be treated. Spend a lot of time on this up front as it will save you heartache and time later on. Remember, people are people. People tend to have filters built in as convenience when people do not wish to give a response. But keep trying even if you have to call up other friends. When there is truly no response, touch back in a few months as some need time. Do not give up on them, but realized you might not be the right person to be their friend. Find the right person who can communicate. If you are not clear about something, it will end up as a tragic misfortune.

One additional note about online friends: online friends are great to keep in contact with, but people still need to know you care about them. Go have dinner, play miniature golf, or take a trip. You will notice that most people will agree that when dealing with people it is all about relationships. At some point if you do this, you will have more than enough friends. But when you neglect them, you will tend to do it because you have other priorities to take care of. But remember, nobody wants a friend to just call them when they are in need.

For example, you probably know a friend who can help you get a deal on a new car, TV, or tickets. But you haven't spoken to this friend in a long time, say six months, the important thing to do is to make the time to send a text a message, e-mail, phone call or even a letter. A friend once gave me a hand-written birthday card. It was one of the best gifts I could ever get because it showed that my friend appreciated me. I can always buy my own stuff, but to get something that normally I could not have is another thing. Spend a few minutes to put together your message to follow-up with your friends as it will pay back even beyond the materialistic things.

We all know the old adage, "Who you know is more important than what you know." As we discovered from this section, you must also keep those relationships alive. Knowing the right person without maintaining is worthless. This is because relationships are keys to successful and happy lives. Genuine friendships complement our family relationships, bringing richness and memories beyond measure. Don't be a friend to someone if you merely would like the individual to help you with business. Build that trust in order to have the business opportunity if that is what you wish.

Yet just like our bodies, friendships require care to remain healthy. It is important to let our friends know that we are still thinking of them. Call them to see how they are doing, not just when you need something. Resist the urge to lose yourself in a relationship with a significant other, at the expense of your true friendships.

FINANCES

MAIN POINTS

- What? Saving and investing money is critical for your success
- Why? If you are occupied with making a living, you can't fulfill your dreams
- When? If time is money, then you need to channel it at the right time
- Where? Finances are applicable everywhere
- How? Seek people with the right skills

"A Penny Saved Is A Penny Earned."
—BENJAMIN FRANKLIN

Many Americans have trouble with their finances because in this country we can easily live beyond our means. But debt poses a serious threat to our ability to fulfill our dreams. In order to balance the Five Fs, it is critical that debt levels stay under control. This can be a challenge in our culture, where so much emphasis is placed on displaying wealth and getting the latest material things.

The first step is to leave behind excuses for not saving, investing, and maintaining a reasonable budget. \With faith that your efforts will pay off, it will be easier to get through that "withdrawal" period. Use your belief that you can do it to help you execute your financial goals, or at least get someone who can hold you accountable.

Depending on where you are with your finances, you have either a balance of a little or in between. Regardless of the situation, you must start. I have a motto about rich people. "The rich get richer because they have time to become rich." What that basically means is that you have to spend the time to look at your finances and ask yourself if you can really afford whatever you are about to buy. You can really test yourself on the day after Thanksgiving on Black Friday. I remember seeing the stores jam packed full of people at the stores buying stuff. I was surprised at the American people because of all the stuff they were buying. I don't know exactly what they were buying, but I do know that they don't need most of the things they were buying. Ask yourself, how many TV's can you own? You can physically only watch one at a time with enjoyment.

It's also ok to reward yourself, but remember that wherever your treasure is is where your heart is. Show me what you have spent money on and I can show you what you have been investing in. Remember, it's ok to spend money, if you can afford it. Don't get into credit-card debit or any debt. If you are already in it, make a plan to get out no matter how painful. It will be easier now than later no matter how much debt you have. Avoid any company that tries to advertise low payments or anything that sounds too good to be true. What ends up happening is they simply consolidate the debt for you and add a fee on top of it. If you owe a certain amount of money, expect to pay it back with interest. There is no way out of it, even if you decide to declare bankruptcy. The companies that have loaned you the money are making it more difficult. Some companies might offer help to employees, usually through a company wellness program.

What to do if you are in debt? Go get help for debt if you really can't control yourself. But you need to get to a point where you are willing to make tough decisions regardless of how painful it might be. Get two jobs, or read books (borrow from library or go to the book store) that explain how to manage money better. Perhaps even outsource the management to someone who cares about you, such as your spouse. There are also tons of software programs that help you manage finances. Remember, saving money is not magic. You must have more money coming in versus money going out. You can make a six-figure salary and yet be massively in debt.

Some useful tips to save money are to cut back on eating out, buying stuff, and going out. As I said before, it's too easy to eat out in the U.S. Besides, it will help with your health as you can choose what to eat. If you are going to eat out, choose to eat an appetizer or smaller portions. Just get water instead of soda or a beer. It all adds up at the end of the day. When friends ask you to go on a trip or movies, just say no. Of course, you are missing out, but it is you who will be paying for everything at the end of the day. Just remember to balance going out because it is important to go to someone's birthday as they have invited you or other special events. Start small because you are asking yourself about changing your habits.

If you have multiple credit card debts, either pay off the one with the highest interest off first or choose the smallest debt first as it will be easier to manage psychologically. Look for better credit-card deals and call up your creditors. I remember one time I simply asked them to increase my credit and lower my interest rates. They did it because I have made my payments on time, and as a result I was identified as a great customer. Remember, they want your business, as you are making them money because they get the money from the merchant. Some credit cards will offer you free frequent miles or cash back. I recommend choosing one or two cards and focusing on them because your goal is to increase your FICO score to above 750, not just getting the rewards. With that score, you can demand better interest rates and terms. All in all, you will be in a better bargain position when time comes.

Want to know how I saved approximately $112,000 through simply refinancing? I remember hearing on National Public Radio one day that there could be a chance that interest rates could fall as low as 4.5 % for mortgages. I thought to myself, I have a relative high interest rate at 6.375% (of course it can be higher). Maybe I can refinance my mortgage. Of course rates were already low to 5.25% at the time. But remember when you talk about a mortgage each percentage makes a huge difference in savings for you. A .25% rate could easily translate to well over $100k depending on the size of the loan. Basically, I told myself I wanted to get the best rate possible out there in the market. So I waited, but I used Google to help me by searching for the best deal out there. Let me explain the exact process that can be applied to other things as well in the financial world.

Google has a great tool that will e-mail you topics everyday on stuff you want to read about called Google alerts. I basically used the tool to search all over the internet for articles relating for that percentage point, 4.5%. One day, after 3 months of getting the alerts, I received an e-mail that said someone got the magical 4.5% I was looking for in the U.S. At that moment in time, I started calling the different mortgage lenders out there. Everyone said, I can get you a 4.7% interest rate, but most people said it was impossible to achieve 4.5%. I knew deep down inside this was a truth only for people that could not see beyond the surface. I kept on looking for about three weeks. On the third week, I was able to achieve the result I was looking for. I got my 4.5% interest rate and saved my $112k just by being patient, thinking strategically, and having the right information at the right time.

At the time of writing this book, the U.S. is going through one of the worst financial crises since the Great Depression. But remember, we made it through this episode of disaster; we can make it through others too. There are Web sites out there like mint.com, or just simply look it up on Google or Yahoo. That will explain what to do. Some people might invest in precious metals or do currency trading. I am no expert with the macroeconomic process, but I am great at identifying what is needed to make your change become a reality.

You might be telling yourself that you are scared to invest or buy anything. The truth is that you must go out and invest now versus later. My dad once told me that I should buy a pair of jeans that I did not need while they are on sale because when I do need a pair I would pay full price. With that basic concept I easily tie the old saying "Buy Low, Sell High" to it. Is the concept not simple and elegant? However, it is a simple concept that most of us tend to not understand. The rich are buying assets now such as property and others while most of us are not. Figure out how to finance the investment necessary to make this become a reality. I am sure you have told yourself like me before, if only I had money I would invest in XYZ. But I simply don't have the money/resources for it. The truth is that most of the time you are right. But the difference between the winners and sideline players is the ones who will write the amazing stores of financial success. You don't have to be a millionaire, but have financial peace of mind. Don't compete for relative low returns; create new value that will be the financial returns you are looking for.

Don't just get a job; get a career in doing something you love. No matter how much you save, if you are making only $20k a year, you will never have enough. Invest in a better career through education in order to get a higher-paying professional job or place yourself in situations where people will offer you more compensation for your services. Don't just hope that you can win the lottery or get paid more for what you are doing. You have to show and bring the value to people in order to get it the value you seek. Remember if you want to take a dream cruise or see Paris you have to have the right amount of resources. The sooner you start the better your chances of success are because, simply, you have focus and better practices than most people. Look for what society values and fill those values. A person who can solve the needs of their society will command a financial stability in that society. What would be quite interesting to look into is a passive income as opposed to active income (your current job). For those of you who do not know what passive incomes are, they are ways of generating money without direct involvement. For example, having rental property is a passive income because someone else is making the money for you. If you think about it, once you have enough passive income, you are done to free up your time to do other things, such as finding new ways to invest in your family, hobbies, etc. The goal is to invest your time and energy and focus what will bring about the most direct return on value.

Many of us will think it is impossible to compete against the market or the big shots for investing. But consider that everyone starts off on the same situation. We all have brains that will allow us to make decisions. Granted, some will have advantages over others, but through perseverance and faith, miracles can and do happen. I would recommend talking with an advisor that is certified at least. It does not mean they know what to do, but they should know something because they do it everyday. I would recommend learning the basis or get someone to teach you. I do have a suggestion that you could take a holistic view of things. Although, professionals will talk about expert or technical advice. But if you can use some common sense, it will go far to compliment their advice. Besides, it will mean you making the decision versus just a random person giving you information. There are some market indicators that can help you decide about when and where to invest. Most of the time, it is based on emotion of the society. Ever wonder why stock goes up or people do when they are optimistic? When people believe it is going up you should invest to get a early start. Commodities will tend to raie in an economy that is going up. When people buy gold or invest in real estate, generally, they are looking for a safe place to put their money to weather the storm until things get better. If you don't believe me, start doing research to get the details. Remember to invest what you are willing to lose, not your money you need at the end of the month.

How do I find the right people to help me with my finances? The right person starts with making a commitment. The other part of the answer is to determine where you want to go. The "how" part of things will come easily because there are plenty of people out there. I would recommend looking for the best person you can afford. Generally, if someone is independent, they will try to find the best deals out there for you. Ask questions and references from other people. Don't settle for what you need, because you are doing yourself a disservice. Some questions to ask would be, "What is your track record? Are you willing to teach me finances?"

Besides, having balanced finances isn't about suddenly striking it rich or making immeasurable quantities of money. It's about being responsible for yourself and your family. Financial success starts with small steps and the desire to control your spending habits.

SUMMARY

I hope that you have enjoyed reading my short book as much as I have enjoyed writing it. Now I know what you must be thinking: It sounds really easy, but I thought I have been trying all my life. It's ok if you fail, but the goal is to keep on going. We would have never gone to the moon if we accepted just orbiting the earth. Keep in mind there were many people in situations even tougher than yours. You are merely playing the same game with new and sharper skills that will enable you to succeed.

So what have we learned? We have learned Faith comes through believing that will enable us to act. Fitness comes from getting up and moving from our comfort zone into physical action. Family will be there regardless of the situation. Friends are important because they compliment our lives. Finances are not about making more money, but managing what you do have to live and share the moments in your life with others.

For all these principles, you must come up with a reason that will motivate you to continue. I found the best way is to have someone hold you accountable. Ask your friends, partner, or anyone who is willing to help you make the habits of balancing your life. It takes several weeks, perhaps even month for you to build the habit. But the earlier you start, the better off you will be in the long run. Just make a commitment to take action. Start with one principle first and build. I have already given you the one to start with to build everything on, Faith.

Go get yourself a notebook now and begin to write your goals, excuses you can give yourself to do better, and things that are preventing you from getting it done. Keep at it night and day until it becomes fluid in your mind and soul. Once you reach that point everything will click. You will see as if you are seeing for the first time. It's the best feeling in the world because your eyes are open and you will feel great.

Now here comes the fun part. I want you to write you name on the inner book cover. Yes, I want you to be part of a social experiment that I have dreamed up because we are about to make changes to the world. I want you to pass it along to a friend, co-worker, or family. You can leave the book on an airplane for the next person. The whole point is that we want people to get better without medication. Also, the reason I want you to do this is because there are so many unbalanced people in the world who simply do not know what causes problems for them. Wouldn't it be great if we could share with rest of the world the ability to have a better life without the need for more stuff?

I want you to go to www.Fivefoflife.com and tell me what you have learned from this experience. I want you to share with the world how great your life is–because it is, and we all make impacts regardless if we believe or not. Share with others on the forum comments, lesson, anything that will help others become better.

If there is no more room to write your name, I want you to keep the book and realize how many hands the book has passed through. I want you to realize that each book has a story because each person who has read it is one step closer to balancing their lives.

You have now become part of a new movement I call *Social Networking* -2.0: back to the human physical element.

WEBSITE
www.fivefoflife.com

FACEBOOK FAN PAGE
Five Fs of Life

BLOG
fivefoflife.wordpress.com

RECOMMENDED READING LIST

The Purple Book:
Biblical Foundations for Building Strong Disciples
BY RICE BROOCKS, STEVE MURRELL

Don't Sweat the Small Stuff
BY PH.D., RICHARD CARLSON

The One Minute Manager
BY KEN BLANCHARD, SPENCER JOHNSON,
CONSTANCE JOHNSON, SPENCER JOHNSON

The Millionaire Next Door:
The Surprising Secrets of America's Wealthy
BY THOMAS J. STANLEY, WILLIAM D. DANKO

Think & Grow Rich
BY NAPOLEON HILL

CONTACT THE AUTHOR

TUAN TA

E-MAIL
Tuan_Ta@fivefoflife.com

WEBSITE
www.FiveFofLife.com

FOR CONSULTATION PLEASE CONTACT
consultation@fivefoflife.com

NAME _____

THOUGHTS _____

_____

_____

_____

_____

_____

_____

NAME _____

THOUGHTS _____

_____

_____

_____

_____

_____

_____

NAME _____

THOUGHTS _____

_____

_____

_____

_____

_____

_____

NAME _____

THOUGHTS _____

_____

_____

_____

_____

_____

_____

NAME _____

THOUGHTS _____

_____

_____

_____

_____

_____

_____

NAME _____

THOUGHTS _____

_____

_____

_____

_____

_____

_____

NAME _____

THOUGHTS _____

_____

_____

_____

_____

_____

_____

NAME _____

THOUGHTS _____

_____

_____

_____

_____

_____

_____

NAME _____

THOUGHTS _____

_____

_____

_____

_____

_____

_____

NAME _____

THOUGHTS _____

_____

_____

_____

_____

_____

_____

NAME _____

THOUGHTS _____

_____

_____

_____

_____

_____

_____

NAME _____

THOUGHTS _____

_____

_____

_____

_____

_____

_____

NAME _____

THOUGHTS _____

_____

_____

_____

_____

_____

_____

NAME _____

THOUGHTS _____

_____

_____

_____

_____

_____

_____

NAME _____

THOUGHTS _____

_____

_____

_____

_____

_____

_____

NAME _____

THOUGHTS _____

_____

_____

_____

_____

_____

_____

NAME _____

THOUGHTS _____

_____

_____

_____

_____

_____

_____

NAME _____

THOUGHTS _____

_____

_____

_____

_____

_____

_____

NAME _____

THOUGHTS _____

_____

_____

_____

_____

_____

_____

NAME _____

THOUGHTS _____

_____

_____

_____

_____

_____

_____

NAME _____

THOUGHTS _____

_____

_____

_____

_____

_____

_____

NAME _____

THOUGHTS _____

_____

_____

_____

_____

_____

_____

NAME _____

THOUGHTS _____

_____

_____

_____

_____

_____

_____

NAME _____

THOUGHTS _____

_____

_____

_____

_____

_____

_____

NAME _____

THOUGHTS _____

_____

_____

_____

_____

_____

_____

NAME _____

THOUGHTS _____

_____

_____

_____

_____

_____

_____

NAME _____

THOUGHTS _____

_____

_____

_____

_____

_____

_____

NAME _____

THOUGHTS _____

_____

_____

_____

_____

_____

_____

NAME _____

THOUGHTS _____

_____

_____

_____

_____

_____

_____

NAME _____

THOUGHTS _____

_____

_____

_____

_____

_____

_____